BIPOLAR DISORDER

Heal Your Mental Illness and Create Your
Authentic Life

(Definitive Guide on Living Everyday With a
Bipolar Spouse)

Joann Utley

Published by Oliver Leish

Joann Utley

All Rights Reserved

Bipolar Disorder: Heal Your Mental Illness and Create Your Authentic Life (Definitive Guide on Living Everyday With a Bipolar Spouse)

ISBN 978-1-77485-090-9

Legal & Disclaimer

The information contained in this book is not designed to replace or take the place of any form of medicine or professional medical advice. The information in this book has been provided for educational and entertainment purposes only.

The information contained in this book has been compiled from sources deemed reliable, and it is accurate to the best of the Author's knowledge; however, the Author cannot guarantee its accuracy and validity and cannot be held liable for any errors or omissions. Changes are periodically made to this book. You must consult your doctor or get professional medical advice before using any of the suggested remedies, techniques, or information in this book.

Upon using the information contained in this book, you agree to hold harmless the Author from and against any damages, costs, and expenses, including any legal fees potentially resulting from the application of any of the information provided by this guide. This disclaimer applies to any damages or injury caused by the use and application, whether directly or indirectly, of any advice or information presented, whether for breach of contract, tort, negligence, personal injury, criminal intent, or under any other cause of action.

You agree to accept all risks of using the information presented inside this book. You need to consult a professional medical practitioner in order to ensure you are both able and healthy enough to participate in this program.

Table of Contents

Introduction

This book contains proven steps and strategies on how to deal with bipolar disorder so that you can help a loved one or a friend who have this problem. In case you are the one plagued with this mood disorder, then all the more that this book is for you!

In addition, this book contains an overview of what bipolar disorder is, how to spot people with this disorder, and how to help them find the balance between two opposing moods that result in bipolar disorder. This book will be very helpful for those who want to understand this problem more.

Thanks again for downloading this book. I hope you enjoy it!

Chapter 1: Overview Of Bipolar Disorder

Bipolar disorder has been an illness that has plagued individuals for thousands of years. One of the earliest recorded studies and observations on bipolar disorder was in 1650. Richard Brown wrote a book called, The Anatomy of Melancholia that focused on depressive episodes.

This book is where depression was coined as a serious mental illness. In 1854, Jules Falret linked depression and suicide together by calling it folie circulaire or circular insanity.   Falret's work led him to   the   discovery   that there is a clear distinction between depression and intensified depressive episodes.

This led him to come up with the name bipolar disorder or Manic-Depressive Psychosis.   Falret's observations also brought attention to the fact that this mental illness seem to be based on genetics, due to the fact that it only seem ed   to   occur   in   certain   families. In the 1960s many individuals suffering from   bipolar   disorder   were institutionalized, due the Congress' failure to acknowledge bipolar disorder as a genuine   illness. It wasn't until the 1970s when bipolar disorder became recognized as a true illness, with the help of some passed laws and   standards.

Different Types of Bipolar

Bipolar I Disorder (Manic-depressive)

Individuals suffering from Bipolar One may experience only one mixed, depressive, or manic episode in their entire life. However, depression is the most prevalent in individuals that suffer from bipolar I. Anyone can be affected by this form of bipolar disorder, and has already affected over 6 million people in the U.S. alone. The majority of these individuals are in their teens or early 20s, and tend to develop in their illness fully before they reach the age of 50. Most people are in their teens or early 20s when symptoms of bipolar disorder first appear. Nearly everyone with bipolar I disorder develops it before age 50. People with an immediate family member who has bipolar are at higher risk.

One may experience extended periods without experiencing symptoms, and minorities are more likely to experience rapidly reoccurring symptoms or depression and mania. Bipolar II Disorder (Hypomanic-depressive)

A person suffering from bipolar II will have at least one hypomanic episode in their lifetime.

Manic episodes are not fully developed in bipolar II as opposed to bipolar I. However, depressive bouts of bipolar II disorder are frequent, last longer, and are usually more severe than the depressive episodes in bipolar I disorder.

In bipolar II disorder, the person doesn't experience full-blown manic episodes. Instead, the illness involves episodes of hypomania and severe depression. These "under-developed" episodes are called hypomanic episodes. Individuals that experience bouts with hypomania are often standup individuals, can often be good company, and can be normally optimistic and inspiring. However, hypomania can bring on unpredictable and dangerous behaviors. During an episode, individual may partake in impulsive decisions and act on them. They are likely to spend money that they don't have or engage in sex with individuals they don't know or wouldn't normally have sex with. Cyclothymia (A mix between Mildly Depressive-hypomanic)

Cyclothymia is a milder episode that involves recurrent mood swings, but the symptoms are significantly less dramatic compared to full-blown mania, hypomania, and depression. This bipolar type and Cyclothymic mood swings go from slight depression to hypomania, and repeats itself. This can last for a total of months and can have an absence of no normal or episode-free period at all.

Cyclothymia can be an overlapping of mental illness and normal personality and mood changes. Some people with mild symptoms are highly driven motivated, and successful individuals, and they use their hypomania to the benefits of their talents. On the other hand, chronic depression and irritability can ruin marriages and professional relationships.

Chapter 2: Traditional Medication For Bipolar Disorder

Medications will be the foundation of your bipolar disorder treatment. Medication can bring your depression and mania under control and prevent relapse once your mood has stabilized.

Tips for getting the most out of medication for bipolar disorder

Avoid antidepressants: Your bipolar depression treatment is different than regular depression treatment. Instead of preventing it, taking antidepressants can actually make bipolar disorder worse or trigger a manic episode. Start by taking mood stabilizers and never take antidepressants without them.

Continue to take medication: Continue to take medication, even if you feel better. If you suddenly stop taking your bipolar medication, your chance of relapse is very high. So talk to your doctor before making any changes, even if you think you no longer need medication.

Add therapy to your treatment plan: Research shows that taking medication alongside therapy help bipolar disorder patients better than taking only prescribed medication. Therapy monitor your progress, help to cope with life's difficulties, and help deal with problems that bipolar disorder is causing in your life.

Natural mood stabilizers: Lifestyle changes has a big impact on your bipolar disorder symptoms. We will discuss more later.

Here are some medications that will help manage bipolar disorder

Lithium – mood stabilizer

Mood stabilizers are the cornerstone of bipolar treatment, both for depression and mania. Lithium is one of the trusted, well-known mood stabilizer and highly effective for treating mania and bipolar depression. However, it is not effective against rapid cycling forms or mixed forms of bipolar disorder.

Anticonvulsant - mood stabilizers

Anticonvulsants were originally developed for the treatment of epilepsy, but they can relieve the symptoms of mania and lower extreme mood swings. Some of them are:

Depakote or Valproic acid: This medication is a highly effective mood stabilizer. The common brand name includes Depakene and Depakote. Valproic acid is usually the first choice for mixed mania, rapid cycling or mania with delusions or hallucinations.

Other anticonvulsant medications for bipolar disorder includes

Topiramate (Topamax)

Lamotrigine (Lamictal)

Carbamazepine (Tegretol)

Antidepressant medications

You have to use antidepressant medications with caution because they don't work well for bipolar depression. Several studies have shown that they have little effect or work no better than placebo. Using antidepressants can trigger mania in people with bipolar disorder. Taking an antidepressant without a mood stabilizer often triggers a manic episode. Also, antidepressants can increase mood cycling.

Mood stabilizers

Here are some mood stabilizers that will help

Symbyax

Zyprexa (olanzapine)

Seroquel (quetiapine)

Lamictal (lamotrigine)

Antipsychotic medications for bipolar disorder

Your doctor may prescribe an antipsychotic drug if you lose touch with reality during a manic or depressive episode. If mood stabilizers are not effective, then antipsychotic medications may be helpful. Often antipsychotic medications are combined with a mood stabilizer for a better result. Here are some antipsychotic medications:

Risperidone (Risperdal)

Quetiapine (Seroquel)

Ziprasidone (Geodon)

Clozapine (Clozaril)

Ariprazole (Abilify)

Olanzapine (Zyprexa)

Other medications for bipolar disorder

Benzodiazepines: Benzodiazepines are fast-acting and have a sedative effect within 30 minutes to an hour. Usually, mood stabilizers need a few weeks to relieve bipolar syndromes. Your doctor may prescribe benzodiazepines to cope with any symptoms of agitation, anxiety, or insomnia,

Calcium channel blockers: Calcium channel blockers were developed to treat high blood pressure and heart problem, but they also have a mood stabilizing effect.

Compare to traditional mood stabilizers, they are less effective but have fewer side effects.

Thyroid medication: Bipolar disorder patients often have an abnormal level of thyroid hormone in their body. Thyroid medication is an effective bipolar depression treatment with only a few side effects.

Chapter 3: What Is Bipolar Disorder?

Bipolar disorder, previously known as "manic depression" is a mental condition that involves extreme mood swings ranging from manic to depressive episodes. These constant mood changes affect an individual's thoughts, judgement, activities and energy levels as well as the ability to perform everyday activities. Symptoms seen on bipolar disorder are quite severe which differs from the usual "ups" and "downs" everybody experiences from time to time. Manic and depressive periods vary from one individual to another wherein some people may suffer short-lived intense temperaments, and might not attribute it to bipolar disorder.

Bipolar disorder ranks second to major depression as a cause of worldwide disability. It often develops on teenagers and young adults. Initial symptoms however, may occur on childhood or later in life. It affects school or job performance, interpersonal relationships and may even lead to suicide. Young men early in the course of their illness, particularly those with history of alcohol abuse and suicide are at highest risk of complete suicide.

Bipolar disorder is a chronic, recurrent condition similar to that of heart problems and diabetes. It is not easy to diagnose early on as its manifestations are often recognized as independent conditions. Months and years may pass before an individual suffering from bipolar disorder is diagnosed and treated appropriately. Although it is a highly disrupting condition, mood swings can be controlled through following a treatment plan. This therapeutic regimen should involve medications, psychotherapy and continuous support throughout an individual's life.

What are the symptoms of bipolar disorder?

Diagnosing bipolar disorder is fairly easy if a person's illness follows the classic manic - depressive mood shifts. Bipolar disorder however can be tricky. More often than not, its manifestations disregard the expected pattern. Depression can immediately dominate the diagnosis while sporadic periods of mild mania can go unnoticed. Other factors such as alcohol abuse may overshadow the overall clinical picture.

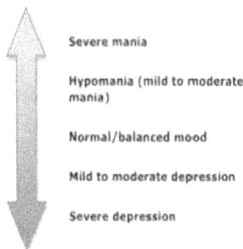

Severe mania

Hypomania (mild to moderate mania)

Normal/balanced mood

Mild to moderate depression

Severe depression

Source:National Institute of
Mental Health (NIMH)

Bipolar disorder causes a range of emotions, which includes severe mania, hypomania, mild to moderate depression and severe depression. Manic episodes occur when an individual experiences a hyperactive, overly excited and ecstatic state. Depressive episodes on the other hand transpire upon feelings of extreme sadness or hopelessness. At times, one might feel manic and depressive in a single mood episode. This is known as the mixed state wherein individuals with bipolar disorder experiences irritability and hysterical emotions at the same time.

Hypomanic episode is the less severe type of mania. Individuals under this state are in touch with reality. They are energetic, euphoric and productive which enables them to carry out daily activities. This seemingly positive episode however causes undesirable consequences as it influences one's ability to make good decisions. More importantly, hypomania is usually followed by depressive or full-blown manic periods.

Manic phase

Signs and symptoms of manic phase include:

☐ Aggressiveness

☐ Euphoria

☐ Overconfidence

☐ Talkativeness

☐ Racing thoughts

☐ Irritation

☐ Hyperactivity or increased physical activity

☐ Shopping splurges

☐ Increased sex drive/thoughts

☐ Carelessness

☐ Risky behaviors

☐ Psychosis (delusions and hallucinations)

☐ Poor job or school performance

☐ Easily distracted

☐ Poor judgment ability

☐ Restlessness

☐ Increased motivation to achieve goals

Depressive phase

Signs and symptoms of depressive phase may include:

☐ Anxiety

☐ Guilt

☐ Decreased or increased appetite

☐ Suicidal thoughts and/behaviors

☐ Feelings of hopelessness and emptiness

☐ Sadness

☐ Tiredness/Fatigue

☐ Difficulty in coming up with sound decisions

☐ Poor job/school performance

☐ Loss of interest on activities previously enjoyed (e.g. sex)

☐ Problems in concentrating

☐ Sleeping problems

☐ Chronic pain without apparent cause

Other manifestations

Psychosis. Manic and depressive episodes can lead to a state known as psychosis wherein a person detaches himself/herself from reality. This includes delusional states where one holds a strong, but false belief regarding a thing or another individual. It also involves hallucinations where a person sees or hears things that are not present.

Rapid mood shifting. Some individuals diagnosed with bipolar disorder experiences rapid mood changes. This symptom manifests itself when as much as four or more mood changes occur in a single year. It is important to point, that mood changes can happen faster (within hours) on some individuals.

Seasonal changes. Similar to seasonal affective disorder (SAD), moods of bipolar individuals may change according to the seasons. Some experiences depression over the fall and winter and then become hypomanic or manic over the spring and summer. This cycle is reversed on other people during the course of the illness.

Bipolar disorder on children and teenagers

Symptoms of bipolar disorder on children and teenagers predominantly present aggression, rapid mood changes, temper tantrums, anger and recklessness. These mood shifts mostly occur at quick bouts lasting within hours or less.

Trivia!

Twenty percent of individuals receiving treatment for depression actually have bipolar disorder.

After the initial symptoms of bipolar disorder, it takes an average of about 10 years for individuals to be treated. Late or inappropriate diagnosis is partly blamed for this delay.

Chapter 4: So What Really Causes Bipolar Disorder?

Based on scientific research, there is a large amount of evidence and reports that point at the occurrence of bipolar disorder as a result of an imbalance in the brain chemicals referred to as neurotransmitters. Despite the fact that the direct cause or etiology of the disease is not very clear, it is well known that environmental, biochemical as well as genetic factors play a role in the causation of the illness. It is important to note that body chemistry in most cases has been attributed to stimulating depression or manic episodes in patients with bipolar disorder. This can also occur due to the presence of other illnesses, hormonal imbalances, stress, and drug abuse as well as altered health habits among others. Additionally, research indicates that bipolar illness is often hereditary and thus runs in the family. Therefore, certain stressful experiences may act as triggers and activate the symptoms of bipolar disorder.

Why it is important to recognize mania

This is something that is very important for you to understand. One thing that most people ignore is treating bipolar disorders. You have to realize that not treating Mania can often open doors to life-threatening situations. Let us examine the case of a woman called Agnes who suffered from mania and was involved in a car accident. Agnes was driving at very high speed because, in her mind, she was a race car driver. On the other hand, a man who had mania invested all his life savings in stock market impulsively and unfortunately lost it all. These are just a few examples of the many people out there suffering from bipolar disorder. In most cases, these behaviors differ from one person to another, but the typical thing is that they are all untreated cases.

Bear in mind that erratic behaviors in itself do not necessarily point to being bipolar. However, if these symptoms or behaviors are recurrent for over a week or more, it is important that you seek medical help from a professional so that you can get an immediate evaluation. The most unfortunate thing is that most people often delay for an extended period of time before they seek treatment or professional help. For bipolar disorder, the average range between the onset of the disease and the correct diagnosis is ten years. This indicates that for as long as the disease is not yet diagnosed, untreated or even undertreated there is a real danger associated with this. This is because, based on research, there are over 20 % cases of suicides reported among bipolar patients who do not receive proper help.

Bipolar disorder in the family line

Despite the fact that the main cause of Bipolar disorder is not yet known, several medical reports and research indicate that the illness is hereditary. According to statistics, there is evidence that demonstrates that 2/3 of people who suffer from bipolar disorder have at least a relative that is suffering from the same illness or unipolar major depression. This is a clear indication that bipolar disorder is genetic and runs in the family.

While bipolar disorders may be considered a hereditary illness, there is not a single way of predicting the manner in which it will affect the other members of the family. This means that if you have such an indication and concern in your family, the most important thing that you have to do is seek the help of a physician. This way, you will have all the questions about symptoms answered and screening for mood disorder performed during the annual medical check-ups. According to DBSA, it is advisable to conduct a thorough screening of all the individuals' health regimen irrespective of whether there is a history of bipolar disorder running in the family or not.

Bipolar disorder in children

It is quite alarming when you recognize the lack of research concerning the onset of bipolar disorder during childhood. The sad thing is that children as young as three years of age have been diagnosed to have the illness and many more children have been shown to exhibit the symptoms of bipolar disorder. More importantly, the symptoms of this illness can be manifested at early infancy. According to research, mothers who have children with bipolar disorder have testified to their children having difficult behaviors and had erratic sleep patterns. In some cases, the children seemed clingy out of the ordinary. Additionally, bipolar children were shown to be uncontrollable, exhibit seizures, tantrums and extraordinary rage from a very young age. In some cases, telling them "no" to something of interest to them would exacerbate their rage.

Similarly, in the case of clinical depression, the first thing that parents have to understand is that whenever they suspect their child of having bipolar disorder, they should immediately seek medical attention for a precise diagnosis. Early and accurate diagnosis of bipolar disorder in children translate to early treatment and thus playing a significant role in the development of the child especially if he or she has a mood disorder.

Chapter 5: Symptoms Of Bipolar Disorder

The symptoms of bipolar disorder fall into two categories, as you probably already know. There are the depressive symptoms, and then there are the manic symptoms. Mania and depression can occur independently or together.

First, let's examine the symptoms of the depressive side. Depression can be presented in a variety of symptoms and signs.

Suicidal thoughts/suicide attempts

Loss of interest in things that used to be pleasurable, including sex

Low energy level

Feelings of worthlessness, hopelessness, helplessness, sadness

Excessive crying

Changes in sleeping habits

Changes in eating habits

Unexplained anger

Unexplained anxiousness

Isolation

Forgetfulness

Living with depression is a daily struggle in itself. Now imagine if we add on the next part of the illness, which happens to be mania. Not only does a bipolar person have to deal with depression, they are forced to deal with these signs and symptoms of mania as well.

Racing thoughts (being unable to "turn off your thoughts" or concentrate on one thing)

Delusions of grandeur (believing you are extra-ordinarily special or even God)

Risky behaviors, including sexual activity, overspending, gambling

Impulsiveness (doing things without thinking about them first)

Feeling "on top of the world" or invincible, leading to actions which may be harmful to themselves or others (high-speeding while driving a car, jumping off a rooftop because you believe you can fly, etc.)

Excessive energy level, inability to rest or sleep

Inflated and irrational goals (believing that you can do anything and everything)

So, one day you may feel manic and the next day you may feel depressed. And sometimes you may experience both sides of the illness at the same time. Mixed episodes are said to be the most dangerous for the person suffering from them. Imagine being torn apart into two extremes at the very same time? It is most certainly not an easy task. It is very hard to function when you are being pushed in two opposite directions at the very same time. We need to find a happy medium. But when depression is running one way and mania the other, it is often harder to get them to join back together, then if only depression ran or just mania.

Despite all the terrible and disabling symptoms of bipolar disorder, I want you to know that you can recover. And you will. You may also be wondering what the cause of bipolar disorder really is. So, in the next chapter we will explore this.

Chapter 6: Why Getting It Right Matters

I hope this little eBook will be helpful as a guide for members of the lay public seeking a very brief and fact-focused introduction to the differential diagnosis of Bipolar Depression and Major Depression. It is certainly not a full exploration of these disorders, and is not intended as such. The professional diagnosing of these major mental disorders is far more complex than could be covered in this small work.

I would be most grateful for any reader suggestions for improvement, clarification, correction of errors, or ways to make it speak more directly to those without advanced training in psychology. I will make revisions based on your feedback.

Bipolar Depression afflicts between 1-2% of the population of the United States. Some researchers using a broader definition of the disorder than used by the standard but controversial Diagnostic and Statistical Manual of Mental Disorders put the rate nearer to 4-5%. That's a huge number of Americans, and it generally holds true throughout the developed world. It afflicts men and women almost equally.

Nearly two-thirds of those diagnosed with Bipolar Depression have one close relative who has been diagnosed with either Bipolar Disorder or Major Depressive Disorder.

Research shows that it sometimes takes as many as ten years for the diagnosis of Bipolar Depression to be made after signs and symptoms of the disorder appear, mainly because the disorder can appear indistinguishable from "ordinary" major depression to the less experienced observer.

To me, the older title of Manic-Depressive Disorder is more descriptive and more easily understood than Bipolar Disorder. But Bipolar Disorder is the currently correct name. Bipolar Depression—one of the two poles of Bipolar Disorder—is not about being just moody. Some people mistakenly say they are "Bipolar" as a way of expressing, "One minute I'm happy, then the next I'm sad, and an hour later I'm happy again."

Bipolar Depression is far more serious than that. In fact it can be deadly. Along with its sibling Unipolar Depression (Major Depressive Disorder), Bipolar Depression can manifest as a despair so deep that suicide seems preferable.

Why is it important to make a diagnostic distinction between Major Depressive Disorder (Unipolar Depression) and Bipolar Depression? Aren't they the same thing really?

In many ways that's true. Yet Bipolar Depression has another "pole" whereas Major Depression does not. It is overly simplistic, however, to focus on the poles, when in fact the range between the poles is better viewed as a spectrum, rather than two dichotomous states.

Treatment of the two kinds of disorders must be different, because treating Bipolar Depression with the same medication used to treat Major Depression can have disastrous consequences.

The primary risk is that a person with Bipolar Depression will be lifted out of depression, but instead of stopping there, goes on to abruptly switch over to the polar opposite side of the spectrum, Bipolar Mania or Hypomania. In terms of consequences, mania can be more devastating to its sufferer, to his or her family and friends, and to the general public than was the depression.

Another risk is being over diagnosed with Bipolar Depression when it is actually Major/Unipolar Depression. In that case, the danger is being prescribed inappropriate and potentially more toxic medication.

Manic behavior is dangerous behavior. Some would say, and I would agree, that Bipolar Mania is the most dangerous of all major mental disorders. At the far end of a manic episode, sufferers can be so out of touch with reality that dangerousness to themselves or others becomes imminent, and hospitalization for the safety of themselves and others is the only option.

Mistaking Bipolar Depression for the more common Major Depression is a grave error in diagnosis. Making the right diagnosis is often life-saving. It is no easy task to distinguish the difference between the two when a person presents for treatment during a deeply depressed phase and no reliable history of previous manic or hypomanic episodes is mentioned to the doctor.

People with either of these disorders deserve our greatest compassion. The suffering is immense. No one would ever choose to be afflicted in this way. It can't be overcome by will power or wishing it away. Sadly there is no cure for this brain disorder at present. For now, treatment is designed to manage the symptoms, and there will need to be close, lifetime monitoring. Bipolar Depression is a slippery disorder, occasionally escaping out from under formerly effective medication treatment. Adjustments in medication treatment are commonly needed. In time, better and more targeted medications will be developed with fewer side-effects and better staying power.

Chapter 7: What Is A Bipolar Disorder? Its Signs And Symptoms

Bipolar disorder which is also known as manic-depressive disorder is a condition where a person experiences mood swings. He or she may have extreme emotions usually from depression to having that extreme euphoric feeling.

People who have bipolar disorder tend to have sudden and extreme mood shifts that other people do not experience. For instance, when you feel depressed, the tendency is that you feel really sad and you start to lose interest in other activities as well. When you mood changes to other spectrum, you feel utmost joy and you have that highly euphoric feeling.

Based on research, bipolar disorder can cause symptoms of depression as well as manila both at the same time. Having this kind of disorder is not disruptive and can be controlled using certain medications and by regularly attending counseling sessions with your chosen psychotherapy. Unfortunately, it is a long term condition that the affected person has to deal with for the rest of his or her life. But the good thing is that there are always ways to have your moods in check.

Signs and Symptoms of Bipolar Disorder

For people who suspect that they might have a bipolar disorder, it is essential that you know the signs and symptoms of this condition to make yourself aware and knowledgeable. The exact signs and symptoms of bipolar disorder may vary from one person to another. Those people who are manifesting the general signs and symptoms are more likely to have this type of disorder.

There are actually various types of bipolar disorder which include the following:

Bipolar 1 Disorder: This particular type of bipolar disorder is characterized by mood swings causing difficulties and problems with your relationships, school and even your job. Manic episodes can be really dangerous.

Bipolar 2 Disorder: Compare to bipolar 1 disorder, this second type is less severe and dangerous. You may experience irritable moments and you may also have changes with the how you function and go on with your day to day tasks. People with bipolar 2 disorder have the so-called hypomania which is less severe.

Cyclothymic disorder: A mild and a less severe bipolar disorder. With this type, the highs and the lows are not as dangerous as the type 1 and type 2.

What is Bipolar I Disorder?

Bipolar I disorder is commonly known as manic depression. This is one type of bipolar disorder wherein the person experience at least 1 manic episode. When a person has Bipolar I disorder, he or she may experience high energy and varying mood changes. This results to abrupt behavior that often leads to certain problems and disruption.

According to experts, any person can have Bipolar I disorder. In fact in the United States, 2.5% of the population actually has Bipolar I disorder. This translates to about 6 million people.

What Are the Symptoms?

When a person has Bipolar I disorder, he may experience various instances where he easily gets irritated and may result to a manic episode. The symptoms for Bipolar I disorder include the following:

Impulsive buying which results to too much spending

Hyper sexuality

Alcohol and Other Substance Abuse

Tend to speak loudly

High and energy level

Suddenly changes their mind

If you know someone who is exhibiting any of these symptoms, it is more likely that the person has Bipolar I disorder. With this type of disorder, a person tend to spend more than what is needed. They also have hyper sexuality where the person may engage in intercourse with people they would not in the first place. The behavior of a person with this condition is also erratic. Albeit just being a Bipolar I disorder, it is important to note that it should be treated right away especially since it may take months.

What is Bipolar II Disorder?

Many who are familiar with bipolar I disorder might wonder what is the different between bipolar I disorder and bipolar Ii disorder. Basically, they are almost similar in the aspect that the person may experience certain highs and lows. The only difference is that compare to the type 1 disorder, bipolar II disorder is more intense since it can result to a full-blown mania. Instead of just having one manic episode, a person with bipolar I disorder may experience having hypomanic episodes.

Compare to the first type of bipolar disorder, a person may experience more at least hypomania. In addition, the affected period will also experience many instances of depression which can eventually lead to manic depression.

In the United States, 2.5% of the population may suffer from bipolar II disorder. There are about 6 million people who are suffering from this type of disorder. Usually, those who are in their 20s as well as teenagers are prone to developing bipolar II disorder.

Symptoms of Bipolar II Disorder

A person who may have hypomanic episode will manifest any of the following symptoms:

Tend to speak too loudly

Excessive energy level characterized by hyperactivity

Problems with sleep

May exhibit erratic behavior

Bipolar II disorder is more serious compare to type 1 disorder as this can lead to an unhealthy behavior. If untreated, this may lead to risky and dangerous consequences.

Cycling Bipolar Disorder

Another type of bipolar disorder is the cycling bipolar disorder. This type of disorder is different from type 1 and type II since a person may have 4 or more manic or depression episodes in a year. However, it is not a permanent condition and can still be treated.

In the US, 2.5% of the population may have this kind of bipolar disorder. 6 million may suffer from cycling bipolar disorder. Basically, this might occur among women. According to experts, individuals below the age of 50 years old may start to develop bipolar disorder. If you have a family member who has a bipolar disorder, you are at risk.

Mixed Bipolar Disorder

Another type is the so-called mixed bipolar disorder. This is a kind of mental illness characterized by varying mood swings and depression over time. A person suffering from mixed bipolar disorder may experience mixed manic and depression episodes.

Who can have mixed bipolar episode? Basically, any person can have mixed bipolar disorder. Those who have bipolar I disorder are at higher risk to experience mixed episodes. In addition, a person who is suffering from mixed bipolar disorder may also experience pure hyphomanic episodes.

Signs and Symptoms for Hypomanic Phase

You might be suffering from hyphomanic or manic bipolar disorder if you are experiencing any of the following signs and symptoms:

Aggressive Behavior

Risky behavior

Talks fast

Poor judgment

Euphoria

Gets easily irritated

Impulsive buying

Sleep less

Inability to concentrate

Aggressive behavior

Higher sex drive

Experiences delusions

Poor performance and attendance at work and school

Depressive Phase of Bipolar Disorder

The following signs and symptoms for the depressive phase of bipolar disorder are the following:

Feeling sad and hopeless

Has suicidal thoughts and tendencies

Anxiety

Have difficulties sleeping

Low appetite

Loss of interest to passion and hobbies

Gets easily irritated

Frequent absences from school or work

Poor performance

Chronic pain

Chapter 8: Understanding Bipolar Better

Your physician tells you that based on diagnostic tests, you have a bipolar disorder. It used to be known as manic depression.

Medicine defines bipolar disorder, or manic depression, as a mental condition where the person who has it experiences extreme mood shifts from delight to depression and vice versa. While the condition usually lasts a lifetime, there are many ways that you can manage the symptoms, recover from the disorder, and continue to live a productive and happy life.

For effective management of bipolar disorder, you have to understand

What your diagnosis is

Why you have the condition

How you have the power to rule over your condition

Crucial to the treatment and management of your condition is your support system. Strong support coming from your loved ones, friends, therapist, and physician will definitely contribute to your recovery. More importantly, you should also realize that you are your best weapon to beat the disorder, and that you can choose to live happily in spite of it.

Diagnosis

Wondering how your physician came up with the diagnosis of your condition? Here is how the diagnostic process works, simplified for your better understanding.

In diagnosing the condition, physicians follow the guidelines contained in the Diagnostic and Statistical Manual of Mental Disorders (DSM) published by the American Psychiatric Association (APA). As a general rule, in order for your physician to diagnose you as having a bipolar disorder, your symptoms should be a major change of your mood, emotions, or behavior.

The following are the standard diagnostic tests for bipolar disorder:

Your physician interviews you and your family member who is with you during your consultation.

Diagnosis is heavily based on the symptoms that you show and their duration, frequency, and severity. Your physician should be able to extract these bits of information from you and your family member.

In certain circumstances, you may undergo laboratory tests if only to rule out suspicions of other health conditions for which your mood change might be a symptom. These are the following: thyroid disorders, brain tumor, and strokes.

Symptoms

Since the bases of diagnosing your condition are the bipolar symptoms, it pays that you are aware of these. Here are the signs and symptoms:

General Symptom:

extreme mood changes that occur in episodes

Specific Symptoms:

Long periods of mania or elation, and similar but longer periods of depression or feeling sad and hopeless.

Intense feeling of irritability, or on the other end, disinterest or indifference in normal activities including sexual intercourse

When you are on your manic or elation episode:

You talk rapidly with difficulty in focusing your thoughts. You will usually jump from one topic to another.

You allow distractions.

You are hyperactive, engaging in multiple activities simultaneously.

You show restlessness and you do not easily get tired.

You find it difficult to sleep at night.

You take dangerous risks.

You have an unrealistic belief in your abilities.

You become impulsive.

When your depressive episode sets in:

You easily get tired and listless.

You suffer from fatigue or lethargy.

You find it hard to make decisions and focus your thoughts.

You have memory issues.

Your usual habits change, such as eating, grooming, and sleeping.

You become restless and easily irritated.

Your thoughts usually wander on suicidal attempts.

These episodes are repetitive and may last a lifetime. With some people, the symptoms linger, while others experience their normal phase in between their manic and depressive episodes.

Types

The WebMD lists five (5) types of bipolar disorder, as follows:

Bipolar I – is the type of disorder where the person experiences his manic episode or are showing severe manic symptoms that may require hospital visit or confinement.

Bipolar II – with this type, the depressive episodes follow a pattern. The person may also experience his manic episodes but they do not reach their peak; hence, the condition is normally labeled as hypomania (failing to reach its full condition of mania).

Mixed Bipolar – is the type where the person experiences both mania and depression in one episode.

Rapid Cycling – is the severe type. The person experiences multiple episodes of bipolar in a year alternating between manic and depressive. Statistics show that up to 20% of those who have bipolar disorder have the rapid cycling type.

Cyclothymic Bipolar – is the type where symptoms are mild. The person experiences hypomania or mild depression.

Causes

Treatment of bipolar, or any disease for that matter, is most effective when it addresses the root or underlying cause of the disorder. As of the present, medical science is still in the process of singling out the root cause of bipolar.

However, the following are factors that may have brought you to your condition:

Genes – your genetic composition plays a crucial role in your condition. Clinical studies confirm that bipolar disorder is genetic. This means that if anyone in your lineage has the disorder, you have greater chances of acquiring the illness compared to someone without a family history of the disorder.

Brain Condition – if there are abnormalities in the functions and structure of your brain, this condition has likely triggered your disorder. In clinical studies involving brain imaging, results show that the structure and functions of the brain of normal persons differ from those of the brain of bipolar disorder patients.

Any of these two factors can make a person a likely candidate for the disorder. Chances are highest for persons that have both of these risk factors.

Chapter 9: The Importance Of Emotional Support And Where It Can Be Found

Friends and family are often the first people to be there to support you through difficulties. If you know your self-regulation is weak then having someone else there can be just the tether you need. While it's difficult to have someone else around 24 hours a day you will often find you have more people than you need if you're willing to reach out to them. Your community around you also will have a variety of different support options that can give you the help you need.

Religion

For those in a manic state being extremely religious can be the solution, but hyper-religiosity can have it's own problems. This is a tough line to follow because falling on either side can be detrimental. Religion is a strong support for those with bipolar. Being part of a community and having faith can be the boost people need when they're down or suffering and it can be the anchor that they hold to during manic episodes.

Spirituality fosters a social connection with others and works on focusing internally which can help improve coping. Faith can provide a much larger network of support and can help with practical support as well. Many offer 12 step programs and uplifting messages designed for those in need. Most adults that are part of a religious community are less at risk for depression. It can also lead to being less at risk for suicide and other damaging behavior because they are against the tenets of that religion.

Author Julie Fast in her book about Bipolar Disorder advocates religion as being something to help you through suffering and that being part of the community acts as a buffer for most people.

Improve Self Esteem

It's especially hard when you're not manic or hypomanic to believe in yourself. During these times when you're at the top of the world, you don't think about negatives and you're confident. It's almost hard to imagine feeling like a horrible human being. Sometimes you even feel that without medications you wouldn't be a complete person. It's just hard.

To improve your thinking during the low times try and foster positive thinking. This way of tackling thoughts helps to turn around the language we use towards ourselves so that we are not so hurtful.

For example, saying you are "worthless" because of your disease is unfair. It would be better to say that you're "struggling". Many of the classifications we give ourselves are actually reflections of other people, but the disease forces us to believe it's our fault. Any classification that uses family, partners, or friends and their faults is actually a reflection of them and their behavior and should be treated as such.

Positive thinking can only go so far, and it's also a skill that can be difficult to master on your own. Using some form of a professional therapist to talk about your thoughts and emotions can go a long way to providing turnaround in how your brain sees itself. Just having better self-esteem can make you feel better overall and is something that should be cultivated.

Practicing Yoga for Focus

Yoga and meditation are great ways to foster self-control. Part of the practice is therapeutic breathing and centering the mind. This helps to keep the mind in control rather than allowing it too much freedom during a manic phase. It's a very cost effective method since meditation and yoga can be practiced almost anywhere. It's also something that can be done independently without a group, though group sessions can help with isolation and building connections with other people.

Using pranayama and asana techniques from the ayurvedic methods have both been shown to improve the way the bipolar mind works. Yoga is a great method for relieving stress, anxiety, malaise, focus, relieving depression, and helping to promote a greater sense of wellbeing. You can even find some studios that offer specifically targeted yoga for bipolar sufferers.

By improving focus yoga can help stop the tendency of the mind to jump off and can help you bring yourself back when it does occur. This means you'll be more likely to practice control when necessary and be more inspired during your low times. The improved focus is key to conquering the manic phase. But isn't yoga an exercise?

Yoga is also a physical exercise, this can help release the same chemicals as any other exercise practice to lift and regulate mood. While many believe cardio = exercise this isn't always the case. Any physical activity counts, so by practicing focus and meditation you're getting both benefits.

How much?

Practicing religion, yoga, and positive thinking are all important techniques to harness your emotions. All of these can help level out the wild swings of bipolar. If you're not a religious person or the idea is distasteful then you should definitely consider the meditations and yoga as an alternative. There are many eastern religions that actually promote this practice which may be more in line with your opinions than mainstream religions.

It's important to keep religious fervor in check. Some people can become so committed to religion that they often lose themselves, also not all religions are safe and some newer ones often turn out to be cults in disguise. Consider any decision to follow a religion carefully and decide whether it truly reflects your beliefs.

Chapter 10: Understanding Bipolar Disorder

Having mood swings is natural; everyone has experienced times when they are happy one minute then completely depressed the next. Now imagine having an average mood swing and then multiply it by several times - that is what it feels like to have bipolar disorder. Sometimes these erratic mood swings can be so severe that it can affect the sufferer's career and personal relationships, and there are even some who have committed suicide because their minds can no longer handle the stress it is experiencing.

If you feel like your emotions are getting out of control lately, and you are starting to experience negative things because of them, then you might have bipolar disorder yourself. You need to understand as much as you can about this ailment so you can get the necessary medical assistance before it gets any worse.

What is Bipolar Disorder?

Bipolar disorder is a condition of the brain which causes recurring episodes where the person's moods will switch from a high-energy, manic state to an almost debilitating depression. These moods are so far from each other that they are considered polar opposites, hence the name "bipolar." These extreme manic-depressive episodes usually lasts for a couple of days or weeks at a time (with normal periods in between them), but in several extreme cases, the episodes can last for months and often results in serious health degradation.

Unlike other mental health issues, it is only recently that people have become aware of bipolar disorder, which is why around

70% of people who actually have this ailment do not get an accurate diagnosis; most of the time bipolar disorder is mistaken for depression, and this actually makes things worse for the sufferer.

Among the people who develop bipolar disorder, most usually experience a depression before they experience their manic state, and some only experience hypomania, which is a less severe manic episode. Two out of three people who experience the depressive state first tend to seek help in dealing with their problem, compare that with the people who experience the manic state first wherein almost all will not even recognize that they have a problem at all. If you think you are at risk of developing bipolar disorder it is best that you get screened and monitored for the condition so that you can do something about it before it becomes unmanageable.

The Different Types of Bipolar Disorder

What makes diagnosing bipolar disorder a bit tricky is the fact that there are three kinds that you need to watch out for.

Bipolar I - This is the classic case of the disorder, in fact, most people think that this is the only type of bipolar disorder there is. This type of disorder is characterized by having at least one manic or mixed episode and usually one depressive state.

Bipolar II - In this case, the person affected does not experience the type of full-blown manic episodes like the ones in Bipolar I. With this type of bipolar disorder, the sufferer goes through episodes of hypomania (mild manic states) and severe bouts of depression. This is the type of bipolar disorder that is usually misdiagnosed as depression because the sufferer does not really notice his/her manic episodes.

Cyclothymia - This is a mild form of bipolar disorder where the person only experiences cyclical bouts of hypomania and mild depression. Most of the time, people who have cyclothymia do not even seek help because their symptoms are significantly less severe than full-blown bipolar disorder, they are so mild in fact, that they do not really affect their quality of life at all.

Causes and Triggers that Cause Bipolar Disorder in People

There is no singular cause of bipolar disorder, and this makes it harder to catch the ailment before it gets worse. There are some people who are genetically predisposed to have bipolar disorder, and yet they do not even develop a mild case of it; this means that besides a person's genetics, there must be other factors that can cause bipolar disorder in people. Researches show that abnormal thyroid functions, a faulty biological clock, and hormone imbalances can also make a person more prone to developing manic-depressive episodes.

And then there are external and psychological factors, or "triggers", that cause the development of bipolar disorder in people, namely:

Excessive amounts of stress - If a person is genetically predisposed to developing bipolar disorder, huge amounts of stress can and will make sure that it happens. It has been observed that in most cases, the stresses involved in life-changing events like getting married, moving away from home, or the death of a loved one can trigger manic or depressive episodes in people.

Substance abuse - Although studies made on the connection of substance abuse and bipolar disorders have been inconclusive, they have been proven to make existing conditions worse. For instance, cocaine, ecstasy, and other amphetamines have been observed to make a person's manic episodes much more extreme, while depressants like alcohol and tranquilizers can make depressive episodes worse.

Sleep deprivation - It was mentioned earlier that sudden changes in a person's biological clock can trigger the onset of bipolar disorder, and nothing messes up your circadian rhythm more than not getting enough sleep at night.

Medication - Certain prescription drugs, namely antidepressants, can also trigger bipolar manic episodes. Substances like caffeine, thyroid medications, appetite suppressants, and other types of medications can actually make a sufferer's manic states last longer and feel more intense.

Changes in the seasons - Seasonal changes have also been observed to cause manic/depressive episodes in people prone to bipolar disorders. Spring and summer seems to trigger manic states, while the colder parts of the year are said to cause depressive states.

Common Myths and Misconceptions About Bipolar Disorder

People with bipolar disorder switch back and forth between manic and depressive states - Although this is the characteristic of having bipolar disorder, the mood swings are often not like what most people assume them to be. Some sufferers experience depression more often and longer than manias; in some people, the manic states are so mild that they sometimes fail to notice them when they come.

Besides affecting the person's moods, bipolar disorder does not really have any other ill effects on a person - A lot of people take bipolar disorder lightly, what they do not know is that it is more than just having mood swings. People who have bipolar disorder often have low energy levels, reduced sex drives, find it hard to concentrate and make wise decisions, and this even causes most people to turn to substance abuse just so they can cope with what they are feeling. Other researches also suggest that there is a connection between bipolar disorders and the development of chronic ailments like heart disease, diabetes, and others.

Besides taking medication, there is nothing else you can do to treat bipolar disorder - Yes, it is true that it is almost impossible to keep bipolar disorder in check without the use of certain types of medication, but that does not mean that it is the only way you can treat it. You can drastically minimize the effects of your manic/depressive episodes by exercising, eating healthy, and avoiding things that cause you stress.

It is impossible for people with bipolar disorder to lead normal, healthy lives - Nothing is impossible, even if you have bipolar disorder, it is possible for you to live a regular, and happy life with the help of proper coping techniques and treatments. If you are diagnosed with bipolar disorder, do not feel like it is the end of the world, there is still hope.

Knowing more about this mental condition is the first step towards recovery. If you have even the slightest inkling that you may have bipolar disorder then it is about time that you seek help, or at least try to treat yourself before your condition becomes too much for you to handle.

Chapter 11: What Is A Bipolar Disorder?

The condition was identified and defined initially as manic-depressive illness by Emil Kraepelin. It refers to a condition with periods of elevated mood that is characterized by abnormal happiness, a lot of energy, irritability, reduction of sleep and decisions not well considered and with no regard as to their consequences, and periods of depression where the patient has little to no eye contact with others, negative perception of life and sometimes outbursts of crying.

BPD results in a percentage of over 6% in suicides over a period of 20 years from the initial symptoms and a 30 to 40% incidents of self-inflicted harm. It is greatly amplified by any kind of substance abuse and if, concurrently with BPD, any kind of anxiety disorder exists.

What is the underlying reason for the existence of the disorder is not clearly understood and explained by researchers. However, contributing factors have been clearly identified. These factors are:

☐Genetic

A mild to moderate effect is exerted on BPD by chromosomal regions and genes that are prone to susceptibility. The risk of the appearance of the disorder in first degree relatives is ten times higher than those that present it in the general population.

☐Physiological

MRIs have shown that there is a number of structural abnormalities in certain brain circuits that may be accompanied by functional irregularities. There is reason to suspect that it is possible that these abnormalities are the underlying cause of the disorder but this has not be definitively proven yet.

☐Environmental

There is a fair amount of evidence that a number of environmental facets contributes significantly to the onset of BPD. Such facets can be:

Recent major events and changes in life and personal relationships

Traumatic and/or abusive childhood

Harsh family environment

Work related issues

☐Neurological

A less common factor is the existence of a neurological related condition like a stroke, HIV infection, porphyria, brain injury due to trauma and multiple sclerosis.

□Neuro-endocrinological

The levels of dopamine which is a known neurotransmitter that is responsible for mood swings, along with gamma-Aminobutyric acid (otherwise known as GABA) and glutamate, significantly increase the chance of elevated mood states.

The neuro-endocrinological factors is the main reason for the need for a correct diagnosis. In some other afflictions like the panic disorder, gaba is a known beneficiary agent when in the case of bipolar disorder it is quite harmful.

□Evolutionary

The theory of evolution dictates that the genes responsible for BPD would have been excluded through the natural process. Yet that fact that there is still quite a large number of patients around the world, suggest that these genes receive some beneficial contribution through evolution.

Bipolar disorder is actually not a single disorder. It is a spectrum of four different disorders:

1) **Bipolar I**

For the disorder to be classified as bipolar I, there must be at least one state of elevated mood to make the diagnosis. Though depression states exist, they are not necessary for the diagnosis,

2) Bipolar II

The characteristics of bipolar II, involve at least one hypomanic episode and one or more major states of depression. The hypomanic episode is less severe than a manic episode (which is what has been referred to as elevated state), and it does not involve psychosis or social / occupational impairment.

3) **Cyclothymia**

This is one of the biggest problems among the people of close proximity to the patient. Usually it is considered as a personality trait and is frowned upon. It involves a cycle of low intensity hypomanic and depression episodes that interferes with the normal everyday functions.

4)NOS which stands for not otherwise specified)

Whatever does not directly fall under one of the previous disorders is included in this category. The only basic common characteristic is that the cycle of manic, hypomanic and depression episodes impairs and affects in various degrees the normal life of the patient.

The majority of the patients that meet the criteria for the BPD spectrum, experience from 0.4 to 0.7 episodes annually with a duration of each episode from three to six months. In most cases there is a remission period between the episodes lasting for about two months. The speed of the succession between the moods is the disorder course specifier.

The traditional medical avenues for the treatment of BPD include psychotherapy and medication in the form of mood stabilizers like lithium and anticonvulsants, and antipsychotic compounds or benzodiazepines. For patients that do not respond to other treatments electroconvulsive therapy may be helpful.

The mere overview and the treatment options of bipolar disorder indicate how serious this condition is. Yet through simple everyday things to do, it may be controlled and overcome so that the patient can have a normal life.

Chapter 12: What Is Borderline Personality Disorder?

Borderline Personality Disorder is among the most prominent of the ten (10) DSM IV-TR personality disorders. "Personality disorder" is defined as a cluster of an individual's long-standing, ingrained characteristics. Such characteristics are usually observable by early adulthood, puberty, or even earlier and result in maladaptive, detrimental patterns of behavior, perception, and connection to others. The diagnoses of personality disorders are separated by placement at a separate classification (Axis II) from most other psychiatric diseases. Other mental illnesses, such as depression, schizophrenia, drug abuse, and eating disorders, are defined in Axis I. While Axis 2 is a long term chronic behavioral disease, Axis I disorders are traditionally seen as time-limited, more biological, and more susceptible to medication. Axis I symptoms usually recede so that people can return to their "natural" role between disease exacerbations. Persons with diagnosed personality disorders generally express dysfunctional characteristics even after the acute problem has been solved. Cure usually takes a long time since it involves changing behavior patterns significantly. Personality disorders, particularly BPD, have proven to cause more severe daily functional impairment than some of Axis I disorders, including major depression.

BPD shares many symptoms, especially histrionic, narcissistic, schizotypal, anti-social, and dependent personality disorders, of other personality dysfunctions. However, BPD distinguishes itself from other distortions in its constellation of auto-destruction, chronic feelings of vacuity, and desperate fears of abandonment.

Borderline Personality Disorder (BPD) main characteristics are impulsiveness and agitation in comparison, self-image, and moods. These behavioral patterns are prevalent, usually starting in adolescence and persisting for long periods. The diagnosis is based on the following nine criteria, according to the DSM-IV-TR (and is generally accepted in the world). An individual must show five of these nine symptoms to be diagnosed with BPD.

Criteria for BPD

Sharp attempts to avoid real or perceived abandonment

A pattern of unstable and intense interpersonal relations that alternate between idealization and devaluation extremes

Disruption of identity: Markedly and persistently unstable self-image or sense of self

Series of impulsion in at least two possible self-damaging areas (e.g., spending, age, misuse of drugs, ruddy driving, binge eating)

Recurrent behavior, actions, threats, or self-mutilation

Affective (mood) instability and marked environmental reactivity (e.g., intense episodic depression, irritability or anxiety usual for a couple of hours and seldom more than a few days)

Chronic emptiness feelings

Inappropriate, extreme anger or problems controlling frustration (e.g., repeated temperature changes, excessive rage, repetitive physical battles)

Transient anxiety or severe dissociative symptoms (feelings of unreality)

As can be seen from a closer look at these conditions in later chapters, the new DSM-IV-TR just underlines slight symptom description revisions. However, the most significant change is the ninth criterion that accepts occasional transient psychotic episodes. This constellation of nine symptoms can be divided into four main areas of treatment:

Instability in mood (criteria 1, 6, 7 and 8)

Uncontrolled behaviors and Impulsivity (criteria 4 and 5)

Psychopathological interpersonal affiliation (criteria 2 and 3)

Thought and perception distortions (Criterion 9)

Changes in mood and impulsiveness are essential factors in suicide risk. These defining criteria were grouped into three categories for classification by a collaborative, longitudinal study carried out by researchers across the country. Since interviewing and classifying hundreds of BPD patients, the researchers reestablished the validity of the BPD-defining DSM variables. The three factors that have been developed are disturbed relationships, uncontrolled behavior, and irregularities in the mood.

Disturbed relationships include self-related and other issues. Identity disruption can lead to relationship problems. When identity insecurity persists, emptiness and meaninglessness often develop—dissociation from reality when the sense of self disappears altogether.

Uncontrolled behavior includes disruptive energy and self-destructive behavior. The remaining criteria include mood irregularity. Instability of the mood also leads to frustration and rage. These intense emotions alienate others and leave the person alone and abandoned.

These DSM criteria define a categorical BPD definition paradigm; i.e., either a person has it (at least five of the BPD criteria are included) or does not (with four or fewer symptoms). This conceptualization allows objective determinants to be measured. All nine criteria, however, are equally contributive, allowing the apparent paradox that someone with the supposedly lasting diagnosis of BPD could suddenly be' healed' of the disease by overcoming even one defining criterion. In contrast, some authors argued that personality disorders that are lasting characteristics should be measurably characterized. This model suggests that personality degrees work, similar to the degrees or rates of addiction. Some authors argue that the condition should be identified in the spectrum by the severity of the symptoms and by weighting other parameters and background information proportionately instead of assuming that the individual is or does not have limits. Consider, for example, that the determination of male or female is categorical and objectively determined by several criteria. Alternatively, men's or women's designations are dimensional, personal, cultural, and other less objective considerations. Proposals for the future DSM-V include a redefining of personality disorders (Axis II) using dimension models.

CAUSES OF BORDERLINE PERSONALITY DISORDER

The causes for this are a complex mixture of genetic makeup, how genes are expressed and interpreted and harnessed under stress, environmental conditions (even family interactions), brain maturation, psychological constitution, and development.

People often ask if there is a brain scan, blood test, or genetic test to identify BPD. Then, there is no such test at this time; however, brain scans and other tests can be used in tandem with measurable actions when diagnosing BPD. It is unlikely that BPD is a single cause, but is instead a result of the accumulation of risk factors in a vulnerable person.

I will clarify this by pointing to specific research in each area. While adults were involved in most of this study, many of them suggest traumas or other causes in childhood or adolescence.

HOW BRAIN STRUCTURE CAN CAUSE BORDERLINE PERSONALITY DISORDER

When we adopted James as a six-month-old, the adoption agency told us that he had a skull fracture, but he had no neurological problems. "What did he do? But he's momentous, angry, and manipulative now. Would you think he may have a brain injury that triggers all his problems?"

This was what a BPD 17-year-old boy's parents wanted to know. If the infant does not grow and then changes in the actions after head trauma, yet there is a direct answer as to whether the behavior changes due to a head injury in infancy, such as James. Nevertheless, as the brain directly regulates the actions and effects of BPD, it is useful to understand brain anatomy.

Some researchers believe the behavioral problems of BPD are in the abnormal operation of the two central brain regions, frontal lobes and the limbic system, and the hypothalamic-hypo physical adrenal axis in one network. We're going to talk about everyone in turn.

- Quick Anatomy Lesson

Our brain weighs approximately three (3) pounds. The brain stem, which contains bundles of nerve cells or neurons, connects to the spinal cord. Most of the cortex is called the brain. The outer layer of the brain is known as the cerebral cortex, which is only a few millimeters thick (such as the skin of an apple), which includes up to one hundred thousand billion nervous cells. The brain is divided into four lobes, known as the frontal, parietal, temporal, and occipital lobes. Each node manages those behaviors.

The hippocampus and the amygdala are deep inside the brain, below the temporal lobe. The primary responsibility of the hippocampus in learning and complex types of memory, and we will discuss the amygdala's position later. The time lobe itself comprises the part of the brain that deals with hearing and sound and speech processing.

The occipital-lobe at the back of the brain includes the visual cortex, which recognizes and interprets signals from the eyes. Our emphasis will be on two brain areas that receive the most excellent attention in BPD: the amygdala and the prefrontal cortex (PFC).

- The Frontal Lobes and Trauma

Frontal lobes form part of the executive function of the brain. It includes the ability to do the following:

• Recognize future consequences arising from present actions

• Choose between good and bad behavior

• Conservation and weight of opposing viewpoints

• Suppress and override undesirable social reactions

• Determine similarities and discrepancies between events

People who suffered injuries or incidents that weakened their frontal lobes often exhibit irritability, impulsiveness, and rage.

The limbic system is part of the brain, which frequently is referred to as the "emotional brain" because it controls many of our emotions and motivations, especially the ones related to survival.

The Limbic System: Memory And Emotions

It is also the part of the brain that monitors the response to combat or flight. The amygdala and hippocampus are the two main parts of the limbic system. The amygdala plays a vital role in emotions like anxiety, rage, and sexual behavior. The amygdala also helps to create memories, particularly memories linked to strong emotions. As Kathleen, a highly sensitive 17-year-old with BPD, began to receive counseling, she appeared dedicated and seduced, but Kathleen refused to speak while her mother attended the therapy. She expressed deep affection for her mother in individual sessions, and her conduct became confusing when her mother was in the house. Her mother said she and Kathleen were extremely close until Kathleen was 14. That was when the mother of Kathleen lost her mother to cancer. She noted that Kathleen was related to her family, but she seemed to have handled the loss of her grandmother as much as possible. Kathleen worked in therapy to experience and tolerate her emotions without becoming self-destructive.

One day in counseling, we talked about Kathleen's theory that the issues had begun around the time of the death of her grandma and how Kathleen and her mom had been very close before. He decided he was close to her parents. "What happened then?"I went to my mother and gave her a hug when my grandmother died. My mother wept and was so angry. As she cried, she talked about her mother, how empty she felt, she lost everything, and now she didn't have anyone. Kathleen said, when she heard her mother say she didn't have anybody, she felt that she was hurt more than ever before. How could her mom believe she didn't have anybody? Kathleen, she had her. She had her. How can she say something like that? Whenever Kathleen saw her mother cry, her mother's memory would trigger that she had nobody. This recollection was tied to powerful and intolerable feelings of loneliness and sadness that led Kathleen to engage in self-destructive behavior as a way to deal with her sorrow. She had never told her mother and had more than three years of suffering from memory and associated emotions. When she was ready to tell her mom, at last, her mother shattered and shouted, "You have been experiencing so long! Why haven't you ever said to me that? I didn't mean I was from you alone. When 14, the amygdala and the hippocampus of Kathleen held her memories of her mother's words, and the autobiography was connected to the feeling of pain, sorrow, and misery. In comparison with those without BPD, the most consistent finding in imagery studies are increased activity in the amygdala, particularly when suicidal thinking is also experienced. It is there crucial to find a way to reduce this behavior to decrease the flow of constant emotions in BPD.

The Interplay

The frontal lobes and the limbic system regularly interact continuously. The problem is that the front nodes, which control decision-making, are shut down in the highly emotional condition, and the limbic system that is involved in emotions takes over. This reaction works against individuals with BPD — or anybody. In BPD, for instance, it is almost impossible to think what the potential result of repetitive self-injury actions, including cuts, during an episode of feeling overwhelmed and self-injured. In BPD therapy, techniques aimed both at recognizing and reducing high emotional conditions are vital. For them, BPD young people can spend more time in their frontal (rational) brains and teach them to manage disputes better.

THE PITUITARY-HYPOTHALAMIC–ADRENAL AXIS

A sophisticated group of nerves that function within the rhythm of the hypothalamus (which regulates the temperature, appetite, thirst, and body rhythms), the hypophysical gland (which secretes hormones and oxytocin — which is essential in the relationship between mother and child), and the adrenal glands (which is responsible for stress) The interaction between these three bodies, through neurotransmitter and hormones, regulates stress responses, governs early mother-infant attachment and regulates mood and sexuality.

Several studies have shown that this nerve network in people with BPD does not work correctly, and therapies for these issues are focused. Some people who suffer from BPD, for example, can take medicines that partially prevent the effects of adrenaline that can reduce stress.

WHAT THE BRAIN REVEALS ABOUT BORDERLINE PERSONALITY DISORDER

Researchers of the University of Freiburg in Germany reviewed the published neuroimaging and BPD findings in 2006. They noted that neuroimaging had become one of the essential instruments for research into the biological causes of BPD. Both imagery and BPD tests showed changes in the limbic system and frontal lobes, which the researchers felt were consistent with the idea that brain disorders contribute to BPD symptoms.

Some people often ask me if any such brain scan or blood test would "prove" that a person has BPD or at least "mistake his brain," as one parent put it. The short answer is that there are no actual BPD exams. The longer answer, researchers look at information from different types of scans to see if differences between the brains of BPD and BPD-free persons can be detected. Such scans have shown to date what researchers expect — that the front lobes and limbic system play a significant role in BPD.

Why BPD Brains Are Different From Non-BPD Brains

The sixteen-year-old Charles, a high school teacher, came into therapy because he had difficulty controlling his anger. He did well in the classroom, but he exploded with close friends and dates when he felt that things weren't going his way or that people weren't fair. He admitted that he had screamed at friends a few times and physically attacked his girlfriend in desperate moments. She is no different from many teens who come to see us because of the impulsive or aggressive approach to others or themselves. Behaviors such as self-mutilation, physical violence, attack, property destruction, and drug use are the only field of BPD that is well explored in science. In a 1996 study of violent and impulsive firing agents, 47% were found to be diagnosed with a personality disorder— especially borderline and anti-social personality disorders. In another study, male domestic violence perpetrators were more likely than men who did not engage in domestic violence to have diagnosed BPD. Brain

111

scans show lower levels of activity in the prefrontal cortex (PFC) in people with impulsive aggression. This means that the PFC is not so active in people with impulsive aggression. Many brain scanning studies show that people with BPD are disordered in the PFC compared to those without BPD, particularly when they also have post-traumatic stress disorder (PTSD). Like I mentioned previously, having a less active PFC means being able to control emotions (such as anger) more difficultly in the amygdala. Ultimately, all neuroimaging research points to the amygdala and the prefrontal cortex disorders in people with BPD. This is yet to be seen whether these anomalies cause BPD or if BPD contributes to these abnormalities.

HOW ENVIRONMENTAL AND BIOLOGICAL FACTOR CAN CAUSE BPD

Dialectic behavior therapy (DBT) theory is that the cause and persistence of BPD are embedded in a hyper-sensitive neurobiological mechanism that interacts with environmental factors. In BPD, hypersensitivity becomes complicated if the person can not control his or her emotions. The biological causes of hypersensitivity may be caused by genetics, pre-born intrauterine, and early developmental trauma, including all forms of abuse.

Environmental factors include all conditions that penalize, traumatize, or overpower this emotional vulnerability and are considered a crippling environment. The DBT model hypothesizes that BPD is due to a biological-environmental interaction over time, which may follow multiple directions. In some cases, environmental influence is higher; in others, biological influence is more important. The result, BPD, is caused by the interaction of these factors so that the person never learns to control his or her feelings while the environment becomes more disruptive.

- Role Of Parenting

The seventeen-year-old mother with BPD who had moved out of her parents ' homes after getting abortion once said to me, "I am so sorry my family is shattered. In months, my daughter hasn't been talking to her father or me. He's furious about how she treats me. I'm still upset with my two younger children. I'm tired and depressed, not thinking that I have much fight left in me. I want to be pleased with my daughter. I'd like to reach her out and help her with her pain. I failed her as a child, and now, as an adult, I fail her. I'm also worried about what is going to happen to other children. "Getting into a" blame game "is not helpful for the treatment of BPD teenagers or their families. There is often a lot of blame on different people when it comes to BPD, and it's easy to get caught in the debate of "bad parenting." In nearly every case, parents did their best. It should now be clear that BPD has many risk factors and causes. That said, parenting will play a part in the development of BPD — sometimes a significant role. Understanding the role of parental education allows us to identify the risk factors and encourages the family to adjust whatever style of parental care contributes.

A recent study found that inadequate parental and traumatic experiences could adversely affect the regulation of mood. The researchers found that people who perceived their parents as poor parents had difficulty describing their emotions and increased depression. However, even if there was also sexual abuse, a positively perceived protective parenting style was found to help teenagers express feeling.

The researchers concluded that the understanding of parenting skills was essential in the development of unable to express emotions. It was also found that one parent's ideal parenthood could prevent the development of alexithymia (incapacity to define feelings, in other words, a person feels) if the parentage of the other parent were viewed as non-optimal.

- Temperament and Attachment

The term temperament psychology is generally considered to be the genetic basis of the personality, the natural, inborn component of a person's character. For example, parents may explain how their children vary and understand these differences in the first year. Besides temperament, a great deal of research and reflection now takes place on attachment deficits in the childhood of adults with BPD. Attachment is simply a desire to seek closeness and feel safe when the individual is present. It is the emotional bond that persists over time and in this particular context connects a child with his mother, dad, or other caregivers. A basic theory of attachment is that compassionate and personalized responses of a parent to a baby's needs result in a secure attachment and an unstable attachment resulting from a lack of such an appropriate response. It remains to be seen whether weak devotion of the parent to the infant is a cause of BPD or whether damaged brain wiring leads to poor attachment. Nevertheless, poor attachment is an almost universal finding in BPD research.

- Parent-Child Bond

The quality of maternal care has been shown repeatedly to predict the safety of infants. The sensitive responsiveness of the parent is regarded as the primary determinant of whether a child is safe. Studies have shown that negative parental personality characteristics are linked to child insecurity. Negative parenting characteristics include, for example, rigidity, black-and-white thinking, lack of empathy, outsourcing blame to others, particularly to the child, and the belief that all of their actions are in the best interests of a child. Research suggests that the empathy and openness of parents to their children make communication with others more comfortable, and that secure connection makes this all easier. A disturbed attachment could have a significant role in the development of BPD. Still, studies have shown, in conjunction with all genetic and neurological results, that up to 87% of patients with BPD who required hospitalization for their symptoms had a history of severe violence and/or neglect and their parents had neglected the 81%. The problem of trauma is significant because studies have shown that childhood trauma affects the functioning of the frontal lobe that is involved in BPD pathology. Nonetheless, it is essential to look at the role of parenting.

Why Early Attachment Is Very Important

Karlen Lyons-Ruth of Harvard Medical School of Cambridge Hospital has worked on the early attachment between infant and caregiver to the later development of personality. She has researched the relationship between first attachment and care quality and adult borderline symptomatology. Lyons-Ruth emphasized the importance of mother-child experiences, which contribute to a child's ability to control emotions. He theorizes that "bonding-exploration equilibrium" disturbance interferes with a child's cognitive and social ability growth. The connection-exploration balance is the idea that if a child is to explore their environment competently, they must rest assured that their mother will be there if there is a threat. A child who is not confident that this will take place focuses on her mother's attachment rather than on her environment. The fear that your mother could not be present if a threat arises corresponds to the fears of later abandonment in BPD patients.

In 1991, Lyons-Ruth and her colleagues reported several studies showing that maternal, family risk factors such as child abuse, parental stress, and the depressing symptoms of mothers consistently produced children who found it difficult to form a safe attachment to their caregivers.

A 2004 review of 13 BPD attachment studies found that each study concluded that there is a secure link between BPD and weak attachment. The most common forms of attachment for BPD subjects are unresolved, anxious, and worried attachments. The analysis found that patients displayed a desire for affection and concern for vulnerability and rejection in each of these forms of attachments. The authors concluded that the identification of unstable relationships in adults with BPD is consistent with the finding of dysfunctional interpersonal relationships with BPD. They also found that individuals with changeable attachments are vulnerable to BPD growth.

ON GENES AND INHERITANCE

Most parents think their child's BPD should be related to their genes, either doing something wrong or passing a bad gene. Also, few adoptive parents know that in adopted children, behavioral severe and personality problems may occur. When such problems occur, parents are often guilty and believe that they are responsible. BPD symptoms–particularly inadequate frustration, mood swings, paranoia/dissociation, impulsiveness, and severe, unstable relationships–are more common among relatives of borderline patients than those of other personality diseases. It also appears that in first-degree kin (i.e., parents, family, and descendants) of BPD patients, BPD symptoms— rather than BPD itself — are more prevalent. Family and twin studies of BPD indicate that while some behaviors such as impulsivity, suicide, mood instability, and aggressiveness do seem to be inherited.

In contrast, BPD itself can not be inherited. Most parents understand, for example, that they are moody as children, but not so unhappy as their infant. Some parents admit that they had suicidal thoughts, but they never did. Given the remarkable variability in BPD behavior, many genes may form part of the complex puzzle. However, there has not been research that found a gene causing BPD; however, studies show that genetic differences can be strongly related to certain behaviors. When combined with brain anatomy and the effects of the environment on a person, these gene variations will provide a complete answer.

Behavioral Symptoms and Genes

The main BPD and genetic research investigated 92 identical and 129 non-identical Norwegian twin pairs. The same genes and the same setting are common to identical twins. Twins that are not similar share the same environment, but do not have the same genes. Researchers found that 69 percent of the symptoms of BPD were genes, and the remaining 31 percent were environmental factors. Most researchers believe that BPD is approximately 60% genetic and 40% environmental.

John Gunderson, MD, and his fellow researchers at McLean Hospital in Belmont, Massachusetts, have conducted an extensive study into BPD genetics. His group divided BPD patients into three subtypes based on the main problems displayed by each group. There are mood swings in the first group, behavioral difficulties in the second one like self-injury, and interpersonal difficulties like bad relationships in the third one. The investigators analyze whether one of these subtypes has a more substantial genetic component than the other. The study hopes to provide results that will help us further classify BPD and develop a gene bank for future BPD research (where DNA is collected and stored). A study of BPD revealed variation in a dopamine gene, the brain chemistry that regulates movement, emotion, motivation, and pleasure sensations. Patients with BPD appear to be more anxious than patients without this genetic abnormality.

OTHER FACTORS IN THE DEVELOPMENT OF BPD

While attachment issues are only a few or low serotonin levels that have had an impact on the development of BPD, there are several parent classes and serotonin booster medication, which are all required.

- Substance Abuse

Dawn Thatcher, Ph.D., and colleagues investigated adolescent alcohol and other adolescent traits as predictors of adult BPD symptoms in 2005. Substance abuse Researchers recruited in their research 355 teenagers with a history of alcohol abuse and 169 teenagers with no history of alcohol abuse. Six years later, BPD signs were assessed in young adults. Researchers found that teens with drug addiction and other psychiatric disorders are more likely to develop adult BPD than teens with alcohol-free mental disorders.

- Sexual Abuse, Maltreatment, and Trauma

Lots of studies have revealed that the majority of people dealing with personality disorders have a history of trauma, neglect, and violence. This is particularly true of people with BPD diagnoses. Adults with BPD and a history of children's and adolescent physical abuse are twice as likely as those without BPD or an abusive account to experience post-traumatic stress disorder (PTSD). Clinicians who treat BPD often seek childhood abuse, and after they find it, they tie it into a patient's cause of BPD. The BPD literature strongly endorses this belief, which indicates that most people with BPD have suffered mental, physical, and sexual violence. Research shows that up to 75% of BPD patients have been sexually abused, and it is essential that many are abused.

Nevertheless, a significant minority has not suffered sexual abuse in childhood. Gunderson found out that sexual abuse is not appropriate or necessary to induce BPD. Evidence has also shown that sexual abuse of a parent is significantly linked to child suicide and is significantly related to self-mutilation, both parental sexual violence, and emotional neglect.

The following listed four factors concerning abuse are essential predictors of BPS diagnosis:

Emotional denial by a male caregiver

Inconsistency in treatment by a female caregiver

Female gender

Sexual abuse by a male non-caregiver

Of patients with BPD who have been sexually abused, more than 50 percent disclose violence both in children and adolescents, on at least one risk factors have been reported as essential predictors for BPD diagnostics. More than 50% also claim that their harassment includes the use of force or violence in at least one form of penetration. It is reasonable that the severity of the sexual abuse reported in children is significantly linked with the overall seriousness of BPD and its general functioning.

Childhood Mental Disorders

Nearly all teens referred to in our McLean Hospital unit were diagnosed with other mental conditions, including anxiety, depression, bipolar disorder, PTSD, ADD, and many others. Childhood psychiatric disorders, such as ADD, ADHD, or bipolar disorder, will increase the risk that the affected child may develop a personality disorder when he or she grows up. This can be done in different ways.

First, the condition itself could directly affect the development of personality. For instance, a child who is depressed can feel worthless, and that feeling can become a core belief over time that they have about themselves. Second, the signs and actions of a disorder can lead to a reaction by others that can impact the development of the personality. For example, a hyperactive child may be physically punished or abused in adolescents by an adolescent parent's 96 Borderline personality disorder or receive different responses, sometimes being punished, sometimes ignored. Thirdly, childhood mental disorder may be in the first place, merely a manifestation of personality problems. Australia psychiatrist Joseph Rey, MD, has conducted various studies over the years and is one of the leading researchers in personality development in adolescence. His group found that 40 percent of patients diagnosed in puberty was later diagnosed with a personality disorder with a "disruptive disorder" (such as ADHM). Just 12 percent of patients with mental (or mood) problems, such as depression, have a disease in their personality. When he continued to follow this group of children into adulthood, the lack of functioning was linked to a personality disorder. Issues included legal issues, poor work records, early coexistence, social isolation, and interpersonal relationship problems.

Other research has revealed that personality disorders are more than double the prevalent in individuals who have adolescent mood, anxiety, and drug abuse disorders, and the more axis I treat a person, the more likely it becomes to develop a disorder of personality.

Online Danger

The internet offers a substantial benefit to society, but there are many threats there, and teens with BPD are particularly vulnerable. Online sexual predators, drug and suicide information, unrelated friendships, the creation of instant peers, and rapidly disseminate anonymous bullying are just some of the dangers.

For instance, research in 2014 indicates that cyberbullying is closer to children's and adolescents ' suicidal thinking than conventional bullying. Cyberbullying today is possible on several platforms, like forums, webpages of social networking (e.g., Facebook, Instagram, Twitter), online games, and text messages. The number of cyberbullying children and adolescents ranges between 10 and 40 percent depending on the age group. A series of articles titled Children, Adolescents, and the internet were published by the American Psychological Association (APA) in April 2006. The APA noted that "75-90% of adolescents in the USA use the Internet for email, instant communication (IM), go to chat rooms and explore other websites on the World Wide Web," and that "much time on the Web can have both negative and positive effects on young people, for example sharing the self-injurious experience with some people, and the academic and health outcomes. The study also found that the frequency and tone of feedback on their profiles influence their self-esteem. Positive feedback boosted the self-esteem and well-being of young people, while negative feedback did the opposite.

The internet can be especially crucial for marginalized teenagers. It offers a place where they feel that they are at low risk to meet others who share their differences (perceived and real) and to exchange information which may be challenging to share in person. The internet also provides anonymity; teenagers can hide behind supposed identities. Studies show that social support and alienation are the principal reason for joining an online forum. Unfortunately, young people with psychological problems are much more likely than without any such issues to share personal information on the internet with absolute aliens. For example, studies have shown that girls between the ages of 12-20 dominate the majority of self-injury boards and forums. You sign in to request and share information on cutting and other self-injurious conduct. True, these channels help marginalized youth socially and emotionally, but they normalize cutting, other self-injurious actions, and potentially lethal "problem solving" solutions.

Anonymously on an Internet forum, the following message was posted: "Thank you, guys. Whenever I go nuts, I sign in. It doesn't even get my buddies. Chatting with some of you is excellent. This allows me to understand, and I am referring to what some of you have done. Having BPD is an awful thing to be treated, and most of the time, I feel isolated. Someone said cutting, but I do not cut. Someone said cutting. Alternatively, I burn and often feel empty, but burning also helps. I have spent all my life in the hospital and emergency rooms, isolating most of my family and friends. I want to find people who share my condition. In an article entitled The Digital Cutting Edge: The Internet and Adolescent Self-Injury, researchers looked at the role of the Internet message boards in the development of self-injurious groups. In 1998, they discovered that a message board with almost 100 users was set up to deal with self-injury. In 2005, 168 boards had nearly 10,000 members. The commissions offered open forums where people felt they were heard. One crucial question is: What happens to emotionally insecure, Internet-based children, or to online lifestyles that provide little continuity or structure?

Who does ask for help when they have difficulty?

Online forums are an impersonal alternative for family and friends. The internet is not full of people who know the situation or the complete suffering of a person who asks for help. One of the biggest fears of BPD patients is loss. For example, if you're online, it's easy to log off when the conversation is too intense. This can lead to feelings of separation if a person with BPD seeks help and the pair logs off online. One sixteen-year-old girl told me if she told a supportive peer on an online forum that she thought of suicide, the person would simply not answer or disconnect. She felt abandoned by somebody she just didn't know. "I've been cyber-dumped," she said.

Nevertheless, the internet offers advantages. Since online forums and blogs can, in principle, be a place where less socially skilled young people share anonymously experiences, they can also be a place for teenagers to connect. Researchers have found that such online exchanges reduce social isolation among youth and enable them to communicate and explore their identity. This will clarify how the internet can become a virtual peer support network for depressed teenagers, a place to express their emotions, and to exchange information about coping methods. In addition to normalizing online groups, self-injurious and life-threatening behavior. We provide a powerful vehicle to bring self-injurious teens together. In the 1980s, anorexia nervosa was commonplace soon after it was revealed as an issue to the mass media. For example, in a 2002 study by Fijian children, disorderly eating became significantly more prevalent after exposure to mass media. Representations of feminine beauty exacerbated it by that emacia. Another told me that when a pair poster, "a mentor," as it was described, told the girl to say to the mother that she had taken an overdose of the pills, it had saved her from the overdose.

Nonetheless, some teenagers say they would never have had the thought of harming themselves had they not heard about it online. In addition to the use of self-injury as a coping skill, many other online discussions are troubling, including alcohol usage, sexual behavior, food loss, and suicide normalization. Another popular topic of youth conversation is disappointment with parents who, they say, do not understand.

Although controlling and regulating the Internet and social media content and access is increasingly difficult, parents and caregivers need to be mindful that these are essential information sources for young people. Some online resources are invaluable, but others are incomplete, misinformed, and potentially deadly. A young person wants a place, whether in counseling or with a parent, in which he or she can inquire about what they read or hear. To parents, curiosity without judgment is the most essential skill to learn. It's an ability that requires excellent practice.

Cultural and Societal Concerns and BPD

All you only need to take a look at any grocery store's check-out alley to see that what you sell is a culture that encourages a' false self' with enamel images, attractiveness over your brains, and sex without engagement. (The false self happens when people are forced to meet external standards, such as to be bad or beautiful, when such expectations can be incompatible with who they really are and how they would typically behave or feel. Otherwise, living in a permanent false self-status can become extremely unhealthy because people lose their sense of their real selves.) One expression is "better chemistry," or the belief that a pill will improve things. While this is very true in many cases, it does not work for many others. Saying to people with the BPD that there is a simple answer or "snapping it out" invalidates their knowledge. The pressure and stress on students (in themselves, parents, and institutions of higher education) to perform and succeed is another aspect in contemporary life that contributes to developing BPD. Most clinics say that self-injury in response to stress is growing significantly.

A major study in 2011 found that of the 11,529 responding students, 15.3 percent registered self-injury, and 6.8 percent had self-injured during the preceding year. Most students who had self-injured reported self-injuries more than once and nearly half more than six times. The average age of self-injury initiation was 15.2 years. Numerous of these cultural factors combine to create the conditions for BPD's growth with the family environment and human biology.

The Bottom Line

BPD is a multifaceted disorder with many components that help to shape it. Research has a variety of links and options. These include genes in impulsive behavior and mood disturbance, have elevated neurotransmitter levels in the BPD brains and abuse victims, and show compromised or underdeveloped areas of BPD in specific brain regions. Instead, the influence of lousy parenthood, broken commitment, sexual abuse, invalidation, drug abuse impacts, and, ultimately, the stresses of contemporary culture. BPD is, therefore, not induced by one factor. Alternatively, the cumulative effects on the developing brain, its structures, and chemistry of the environment and the genes draw together the clinical picture.

The downside is that BPD develops over time and often needs years of healing therapy. Nonetheless, it is promising that there are several approaches, and these interventions will continue to improve over time.

Chapter 13: Is Good Communication Possible?

Almost every expert on relationships advocates good communication as an essential ingredient for a rewarding and lasting relationship. It is through such communication that couples can attain a genuine understanding of each other and define both individual and shared goals. The capacity to freely and honestly share one's thoughts and feelings with a loved one reflects a deep level of trust and intimacy that is the foundation for a lasting commitment. But what exactly is "good communication"? And, more significantly, what challenges may you experience while trying to foster good communication with your partner who has bipolar disorder?

All Relationships Have Communication Issues

Almost everyone at some time finds it difficult to speak with another person. Such difficulty goes beyond asking your boss for a raise or confronting your overbearing mother-in-law. Sometimes it can seem like an act of courage just to ask your partner to turn the volume down on the television. Not because your relationship is abusive, but because the unspoken dynamics of your bond emerge between you and your partner over time: "Will I sound like a nag if I bring this up again?" or "Will I hurt his feelings if I tell him I don't eat veal?" At times, even thinking of expressing the smallest concern may lead to anxiety.

You may also believe that, in some way, you are the caretaker in your relationship and your needs are less relevant. You may view your bipolar partner as someone you need to nurture but who is not available to meet your needs. Perhaps you're driven by some underlying discomfort with being nurtured based on not wanting to feel weak and in need of support. Your role as caretaker may also derive from a genuine fear that you won't be able to depend on your partner to be there for you if and when you need him.

Without full awareness, your communication difficulties may stem from your need to maintain negative feelings toward your partner. This may be the case if, for example, over time you resent the sacrifices you make or if, by overlooking your own needs, you increasingly feel isolated and alone in your relationship. Harboring negative feelings toward your partner may serve as a distraction from the real disappointments that you experience in the relationship. In the extreme, you may start to believe your partner is a bad person and, by confirming this belief, you don't need to work at making things better. Although unaware of any subconscious desire, the subliminal need to maintain resentment may actually facilitate the task of ending a bad relationship.

Communicating Anger

In any relationship, it is often challenging to know when to say what without making a bad situation worse. This can be especially true in a bipolar relationship. Emotions can greatly override how we interpret what we hear. Perhaps you'll be greeted with a favorable response, but other times your comment may cause negative emotions in your partner, creating tension for both of you. At times, you may have hindsight about how you contributed to your partner's reaction. On other occasions you may have no clue as to how your comments could have had such a negative impact. Since nobody is perfect, we are all guilty at one time or another of saying something that our partner may not respond to as we might have hoped.

Part of the challenge in communicating is based on the fact that maintaining a healthy relationship involves some degree of compromise in order to preserve each partner's individual identity. It's reasonable that two individuals will need to address and share their unique perspectives and expectations as they work on their relationship. Because bipolar illness can involve impairment in judgment and emotion, what you say may not be heard as you intended and can subsequently arouse tension for both of you. As in any relationship, an occasional argument is normal — and actually improves communication — since it would be unrealistic to expect persons living together never to be in conflict. However, if arguments are frequent and pervasive you may need to consider couples counseling as a way of developing techniques to help you better communicate.

The discomfort many people experience with any form of anger is another factor that undermines candid communication, and the stress of coping with bipolar disorder can make both of you especially sensitive to this complex and challenging emotion. Too often people associate anger with rage or aggression. Rage can be scary for other people to witness, as the raging person seems out of control and unpredictable. It may be especially difficult for your bipolar partner to observe you in such a state and just as difficult for you if your partner appears to be enraged. Even when no one is physically injured, the sheer force of the rage can deeply wound the souls of those exposed to it. Nearly all anger is the reaction to other negative emotions, such as anxiety, shame, disappointment, frustration, or the feeling of being devalued or rejected. An honest relationship requires partners to directly communicate feelings of anger with each other. Direct communication of anger means sharing the feelings that lead to anger as well as the anger itself. It means talking about the anger and not "showing" it in angry behavior. You would, for example, be candid and direct by saying, "I am disappointed and become anxious when you do not take your medication. That makes me irritated."

Case Study: Mike and Pat

Effective communication often requires patient self-reflection in order to identify what it is that you want to express. Mike, a forty-two-year-old married man, sought counseling at the request of his wife because of his increasing episodes of anger, which had escalated during the past several months. While Mike had a history of periodic verbal outbursts, he was becoming abusive in his language and, on several occasions, frightened his wife, Pat, a woman with a history of bipolar illness.

Mike initially focused much of his anger on his wife for a variety of issues that often related to the symptoms of her illness. In therapy, he learned to identify the negative emotions that fueled his anger when Pat hadn't behaved as he believed she "should." While initially only able to recognize his anger, he soon was able to acknowledge disappointment, frustration, a sense of inadequacy, and feelings of being powerless to impact his wife. Mike also admitted to personal disappointment and frustration for his inability to be more effective in helping Pat. Additionally, he experienced some levels of shame that accompanied his perceived failures.

Much of Mike's anger was related to his expectations regarding Pat's behavior and his ability to influence it. To address this, he was helped to clarify the ways he could control the situation and also when he could not impact change. At the same time, Mike became mindful of how he had personalized Pat's behaviors. On many occasions, when she was distracted by her symptoms, Mike was quick to conclude that Pat did not care for him or respect him. Instead, he learned to expect and accept that there would be times when Pat might not be fully present and considerate of him. Most significantly, he learned to be cognizant that his intense anger was, in reality, a revisiting of long-held feelings of not being cared for, which he had experienced years before his marriage. Through this realization, he was able better clarify what was important to communicate to Pat so she could more readily understand him when she was ready to listen.

"Good" communication requires hard work and never comes easy. It may even involve venturing into the unpleasant and difficult; but, it does not require excessive, annoying, or constantly probing communication. If you say, "I think I'll get a glass of water," and your partner says, "What do you mean by that?" your partner needs to lighten up. Good communication entails a shared sense of humor, mutual and good-natured teasing, and sometimes just a few words of encouragement.

In a relationship with a bipolar person, it might be useful to remember that no relationship has "perfect" communication and that many of the challenges you face are the same as in any loving relationship. Still, some challenges to effective communication are unique to a relationship when one of the partners has bipolar disorder.

The Elephant in the Room

The fact that your partner has bipolar disorder can never be fully ignored in regard to its potential impact on your communication. If your partner has an excellent response to treatment, it may have little if any effect on the communication in the relationship even though your awareness of the illness may play a role in how and when you bring up certain issues. However, if treatment is only partially successful, or if your partner is not on medication therapy or in the middle of a manic or depressive episode, then complications may emerge to confound the communication process.

Will My Partner Have an Episode?

Even if your partner appears stable in his moods, you may be afraid that bringing something up will trigger an episode. You may fear that any news, even good news, may trigger mania. Conversely, you may fear that bad news will lead to serious depression. Beyond a certain point you must let life unfold, and your partner has the right to know the facts. If you are still concerned about the potential response to what you need to communicate, seek a professional for advice or to be present when you confront your partner. If the issue is less serious, go ahead and tell your partner that you wrecked the car, got a huge raise, that she hogs all the blankets at night, or whatever it is you want to say.

Will My Partner Be Too Out-of-It to Care?

At the other extreme, your partner's medication regime may tend to make him feel flattened out emotionally and unable to react to your news. Sometimes the need for medicating symptoms is so great that the bipolar patient cannot do anything other than stay home and watch television. Even if he holds down a job he may seem out of touch or unable to remember what you tell him.

For example, let's say you just found out something tragic: your brother was in a car accident and is in serious condition. You really want your partner to be there for you — to listen, to hold you, to bring you real comfort. While your bipolar partner may usually be able to do all this, the impact of his medication may make him unavailable to provide you any emotional support. He may even seem hurtful at such moments. You state that your brother is in the hospital, and your partner replies, "Gee, that's too bad. I'm sorry to hear it. What should we have for dinner?"

WORD TO THE WISE

Do Unto Others

You know how challenging it can be when someone wants to initiate a conversation when you are transitioning from one activity to another. Such moments may even be more difficult for your partner. For example, when you walk in the door following a full day's work, you may prefer time out to get settled before being confronted with your partner's wish to discuss vacation plans. Nevertheless, your bipolar partner deserves equal consideration.

At such moments, you need to remember that the illness, perhaps in combination with the side effects of the medication, undermines his capacity to be fully present

157

and positively responsive. It may be useful to drop a small hint, or be very specific, to assist your partner in focusing his attention. This may push you beyond your comfort level, but it may be necessary to directly ask: "Would you please hold me for a while?"

Will My Partner Be Too Self-Absorbed to Care?

When medication is only partially effective, or if your significant other isn't on medication, there may be moments of mania and depression that compete with your need to communicate. If your partner is manic, she may seem extremely agitated, as if she just drank ten espressos in a row. She may not sit still or may speak so quickly and so forcefully that you're unable to reply. In this frame of mind, she may think nothing of interrupting you in midsentence and changing the topic. This incomprehensible monologue goes nowhere and everywhere simultaneously. Moreover, in this frame of mind your partner may seem to have little regard for your feelings and be extremely blunt and hurtful without even knowing it.

For example, after speaking with your sister on the telephone, you may report to your partner, "I feel terrible. Cathy and Brian are getting divorced." Your partner replies, and does it so rapidly that you can barely comprehend let alone interject, "Well, I saw it coming. Didn't you? They really weren't right for each other. I know they went to counseling, but I didn't think that could fix it. Speaking of fixing, I've been trying and trying to get someone over here to look at the leaky faucet. I got seven estimates today, but none of them were any good. I've been thinking anyway, maybe we should just remodel the kitchen. I saw some great ideas in the magazine." And so on.

Case Study: Ann and Mark

Ann and her husband Mark were collaborating on a children's book, but Mark frequently needed to remind Ann to slow down, take a break, and refocus. He states, "She writes for hours without coming up for air. Then, she wants my undivided attention, but it's always on her timetable. She will complete a chapter and present it to me as a 'fait accompli,' and I sometimes find myself pulling away. I know that these signs are symptoms of Ann's bipolar condition, but it's difficult to deal with her when she's so off-balance. She expects me to drop everything and listen, and her fixation is reflected both in her tone and rate of speech as if something big is about to happen. There's an aura of excitement about her, but as we sit for long periods I feel disjointed, somehow distant, like I'm viewing a special effects scene at a movie theater. I'm drawn into the drama, yet not fully a part." During periods of self-reflection, Ann admits that Mark seems edgy when she confronts him on these occasions. Mark's response:"She rambles on and on, which leaves me with a twinge of sadness. I find myself asking, Is it me? Or, is it something about Ann?"

In time, Mark began to grow weary of Ann's apparent highs and lows and, likewise, she became increasingly disenchanted by what she considered to be Mark's insensitivity to her affliction. The dilemma so exacerbated Ann's distress that her self-confidence eroded to a temporary new low.

When Ann and Mark reached the final editing stages of the book, their work pace quickened. She telephoned Mark at his office more regularly during this period, and he felt her calls were all about "trivial details unrelated to the book." Ann says, "Mark complained that my messages carried a sense of urgency and that my points were sometimes repetitive. When Mark did not immediately pick up the call, I left messages. I am accustomed to replying quickly to telephone messages, faxes, and e-mail correspondence. Mark, on the other hand, does not. He gives himself what he considers 'a comfortable window for response,' which works for him but annoys me. It seemed clear that Mark and I had different ideas about what is 'important.' My manner of dealing was to wait an hour or two and if he didn't call or e-mail back, I sometimes repeated the message if I felt it was important and could not wait. Is it possible, I thought, that heightened tension has prompted

Mark to hold the relationship with me at bay by keeping it narrowly defined? He had apparently begun to distance himself.

"Finally, Mark attempted to structure our conversations about the book so they did not exceed ten to fifteen minutes. I found this restriction exasperating. 'What's your goal, Ann?' Mark would ask. Frequent clashes resulted because it is difficult and unnatural for me to talk 'bottom line.' I envisioned an imaginary time clock, and in order to get in all my thoughts I began to talk faster and faster."

Several months after Mark and Ann had completed working on their book, he described his thoughts in a short personal essay: "Ann is speaking louder and faster. Her voice is strident, the sweetness gone. How does she have time to breathe between words? She accuses me of being critical of her. I feel I am not being heard.

In frustration, I put down the phone and walk away. When I return a few minutes later, Ann is still talking; she did not even notice my absence.

It's Tuesday afternoon and my answering machine is blinking to be played. My e-mail box is full with messages sent by Ann. I let out a sigh and ignore them. Many times there is no new information. Or I receive six e-mails all the same, each addressed to a different recipient on which I am copied."

Over a period of months, Ann and Mark's relationship eroded further and they kept each other at a comfortable distance. Ann worried about their marriage ending since the tension between them had heightened. Mark was setting limits and beginning to apply the brakes. In looking back, Ann can now see how Mark's frustration over this matter must have heated up to the point of actual boiling. But she, too, was at the brink of explosion. Both are strong willed individuals with different priorities and working styles that just didn't mesh. What kept them together was the strength of their bond and a mutual desire to work through their problems.

When you care about your bipolar partner, it's possible to see the light side of her personality while being accepting of her quirkiness. Nevertheless, it can be exasperating in the moment, especially if you are unaccustomed to this kind of reaction. At such times, try to remember that it's the mania — the illness — talking. Be prepared to bring up whatever you have said again because your manic partner is likely to forget what you said. You may even consider putting off addressing the subject until things calm down. But if things do not settle down soon, or if what you need to communicate cannot wait, try to re-create the scene to emphasize the importance of what you want to say. Keep the conversation brief.

For example, you may try to make your partner think that listening to you is his ultimate task of the moment: "I have to ask a favor. I need to say something very important because I trust you, and I need you to sit down with me and listen." Physical contact, such as clasping hands, maintaining eye contact, and speaking slowly in a modulated tone of voice may also help to emphasize the urgency of your message. Since your partner is in a very active mode, he may welcome the chance to do something for you. Next, you might add: "I only have a few minutes to talk, so I need to just say it." Wait briefly for a response. Based on your partner's reaction, you may decide to continue speaking or just thank him for listening and end the conversation.

If your partner is feeling depressed, he may not welcome your conversation and may instead appear moody and disinterested. If you think you can snap him out of his depression by sharing bad news of your own, you should reconsider. His depression stems from a serious illness and cannot be diffused by subtle strategies. Nor will small talk aimed at changing the subject distract him from his own unhappiness.

What may seem evident needs emphasizing: nobody enjoys being depressed. If a depressed person could merely "snap out of it," he would. This may be especially difficult to remember when you unrealistically expect that your partner will be more fully present with you. Understandably, you may be prone to frustration when he refuses to go to a movie or follow through with a simple house chore or must be coaxed to get out of bed.

Hopefully, a professional is monitoring your partner's depression so, for now, keep communication with your loved as straightforward as possible. Some things will need to be shared, and you should, by all means, listen to your partner if she wants to talk about the depression with you. You may even want to gently approach the subject yourself, and remind her how much you care. Without a gentle reminder, she may erroneously conclude that you are angry, don't want to discuss the issue, or have given up on her. Whatever the situation, it is the wrong time to expect any kind of mutual give and take. When your partner's depression becomes severe, you may question her feelings toward you — did she ever did care? Do what you can to help, talk to your loved one's doctor, and re-evaluate the situation when the depression lifts. What appeared to be disinterest was likely a symptom of the depression that took away all sense of your partner's joy. Once she feels better, her love for you may well be intact.

Don't Forget Your Own Needs

When your partner is manic or depressed, it's probably not the best time to sit down and discuss the state of your relationship, but what if it seems like there's never a good time? Is it just the bipolar disorder or are there other factors involved?

Some people naturally shy away from revealing too much information about themselves, especially concerning their relationships. Others chatter incessantly but talk about nothing deep or serious.

They may feel uncomfortable and self-conscious or may not be fully in touch with their feelings. Others may harbor fears and insecurities unrelated to their bipolar condition. Perhaps, for example, your partner comes from a family that demonstrated very little love and acceptance, or where the children were denied the ability to express how they felt. Consider your partner's background. What are her family members like? Do her siblings also complain about personal problems, even though they are not bipolar? Do you also dislike her parents?

ASK THE DOCTOR

Does everyone get depressed?

Rare is the person who never feels depressed and, since emotions are contagious, you may find yourself experiencing some level of depression along with your partner. If the condition persists, seek professional help. However, your own experience may help you respond to your bipolar partner. If you find yourself losing patience, try remembering a time when you felt low. Did you feel hopeless, as though nothing could ever make you feel good again? Empathy is important to all relationships.

Always remember that people — bipolar or not — may have many reasons for not being good communicators. If their condition is unrelated to bipolar disorder, you may decide that something needs to be done. With the guidance of a professional, you may explain to your partner that you feel the two of you never really talk and that you want to correct this because you want to feel closer to him. If the bipolar symptoms seem responsible for the communication difficulties, in part because of treatment, express these concerns in a professional setting, as well.

Should little change over time, even with the help of a professional, you may want to explore your options. Some people grow to accept that their partner is not a good communicator but feel that the relationship is still satisfying. Others begin to feel lonelier than before they became a couple. If you have tried every avenue and your needs are not being met, consider your alternatives.

When It's Hard to Talk to Your Partner

We have identified many scenarios in which bipolar disorder, its treatment, and related factors can limit communication. In the following discussion, we highlight several patterns of reaction that you may fall into when dealing with communication difficulties. We encourage you to be mindful of falling into such patterns and offer strategies to avoid the pitfalls.

The Fake Happy Person

You may find yourself unwittingly gravitating toward fake happiness when your partner is depressed. Without full awareness, couples often embark on a division of labor for all aspects of their life. Simply put, if one of you is unhappy, the other might feel compelled to act happy in order to balance things out. However, happiness may be difficult when the person you love is sad. You're probably worried about what comes next: Will this all-pervasive gloom never end? Will he need hospitalization? Will there be a suicide attempt?

Due to these worries, the "happiness" you display probably feels insincere. In fact, your facade of happiness may be unsettling to you and to others because its lack of authenticity creates tension. Your partner may also feel it. Depressed as he is, your partner may inform you in rather harsh terms how he feels about your "mask" of happiness. While you're trying to remind your partner that life holds goodness and beauty, your timing is off since you're neither seeing nor feeling what you profess as fact. No matter how good your intensions, nobody likes a phony.

Be mindful of maintaining realistic expectations while remaining determined to survive your partner's depression. Also, do whatever possible to make sure he is getting the best professional help possible. Simultaneously, seek out support groups for yourself or confide in people whom you trust to respect your feelings. Allow yourself to be sad or cheerful as the mood strikes you, and remember that nobody benefits from a lack of authenticity.

WORD TO THE WISE

It's Okay to Cry

If your partner wants to cry, even seemingly about nothing, let it happen. You may even find yourself in tears. Crying is an emotional release, but additional counseling for your partner may be justified if she is sobbing uncontrollably.

The Pipsqueak

When your partner is manic and barely lets you interject a word while busying himself with matters of no concern to you or, perhaps, involves you against your wishes, you may feel like a pipsqueak — something small and insignificant, yet annoying. In reaction to your partner's overwhelming (and at times overbearing) emotionality, you may experience a kind of age regression where you feel like the only child in a roomful of grownups. This experience may lead you to tap into the kind of loneliness or frustrating sense of insignificance that you may have felt as a child. As that child of your youth, you maybe felt paralyzed to speak up and protect yourself, so you found passive-aggressive ways of making your displeasure known. Today, you may act moody, hoping that someone asks what is wrong, but no one does. Even if someone does inquire, you make the fatal error of answering "nothing," rather than availing yourself of the opportunity for some honest communication. But, given the way you feel, you cannot speak up.

If you're in this state of mind, it may be best to go off in your own direction to regain your full adult sense of self. However, you may feel the need to remain close by in case the situation gets out of hand or you may not be able to bring yourself to disengage. In such a state, you may experience a sense of paralysis, feeling you deserve to be belittled and ignored, so you passively react to your discomfort. For example, you may tag along with your manic partner while she goes on a shopping spree while never asking if there is anything you want to look at or purchase. Perhaps you think you have a better chance of keeping expenses down by being there — and maybe you can — but be careful that you don't get yourself into trouble by going along with your partner's impaired, manic judgment.

Although you may be steaming in silent resentment, vowing never to accompany your partner again or perhaps considering a break-up — anything other than accompanying your partner in the moment — stay put! Sharing your dissatisfaction in a compassionate manner will be better for both of you.

The Copycat

While partners sometimes seek to balance each other, at other times they want to copy each other. It is not unusual for people in a relationship to acquire a taste for a food or style of music enjoyed by their partner. Perhaps her hobby now becomes your hobby, or his favorite vacation place is now your favorite. The propensity to adopt the likes and dislikes of a partner is a natural reaction of being in a close relationship, much the same as children who discover new ways from parents or friends.

Even if you disagree politically or maintain different religious beliefs, over time you'll probably empathize with your partner's point of view. Sometimes things go a step further, and one party converts to the other's religion or political party. Perhaps you never got angry about environmental issues until your partner instilled you with anger. Or, you take your partner's side in a dispute with a third party even though that might not have happened had you been single.

Many partners adopt each other's moods and feelings, but this phenomenon takes on a special meaning in a relationship with a bipolar person. Although you cannot become bipolar, you may innocently get into the manic or depressed mood of the moment. For example, if your partner is depressed and moping about the house, or sleeping or eating too much or too little, you may feel compelled to imitate his behavior: if he's not hungry, neither are you; he feels tired, so do you; he doesn't want to venture out, so neither do you. You agree that life stinks. If your partner is manic, you are having the best time in the world in his company. You laugh, go places, and do things. You may even join your partner in binge drinking or overspending.

At such moments, mirroring your partner may derive from your wish to feel closer and more united. Again, you cannot will yourself to be bipolar, but perhaps you can empathize or identify with your partner's extreme high or devastating low. In this situation your strength in empathizing has led to "empathy gone awry" and you may now be unable to step back and view your partner objectively.

These are not wise behavioral choices to make. Mania and depression harm the self on many levels, and your own lighter, semi-genuine versions of these feelings can cause you personal harm. Take good care of yourself, and remember that entering into a world of unwise choices is unhealthy and can be dangerous.

Good communication helps foster trust in a relationship, and building and maintaining trust is the prerequisite to promoting honesty and directness in communication. In the following chapter, we will highlight those factors that deserve attention in establishing a relationship based on trust with your bipolar partner.

Conclusion

Thank you again for downloading this book!

I hope this book was able to help you to understand more about bipolar disorder.

The next step is to take action on how to live life happily despite having this disorder. Help your friends, help your loved ones, and help yourself.

Thank you and good luck!